**Earning, Saving, Spending**

# Credit Cards and Checks

## Margaret Hall

**Heinemann Library**
**Chicago, Illinois**

© 2000 Reed Educational & Professional Publishing
Published by Heinemann Library,
an imprint of Reed Educational & Professional Publishing,
100 N. LaSalle, Suite 1010
Chicago, IL 60602
Customer Service  888-454-2279
Visit our website at www.heinemannlibrary.com

Designed by Depke Design

04 03 02 01
10 9 8 7 6 5 4 3 2

**Library of Congress Cataloging-in-Publication Data**
Hall, Margaret, 1947-
          Credit cards and checks / Margaret Hall.
                    p. cm. - (Earning, saving, spending)
          Includes bibliographical references and index.
          Summary: An introduction to checks, credit cards, and debit cards, explaining
how they work and why people use them.
          ISBN 1-57572-232-1 (library binding)
          1. Checks-Juvenile literature.  2. Credit cards-Juvenile literature.  Debit
cards-Juvenile literature  [1. Checks.  2. Credit cards.  3. Debit cards.  4. Finance, Personal.]  I Title.
HG 1691.H32  2000
332.76-dc21                                                            99-046697

**Acknowledgments**
The author and publishers are grateful to the following for permission to reproduce copyright
material:

Cover photographs: Stock Boston/Bob Daemmrich (top), International Stock/Patrick Ramsey,
(bottom).
International Stock/Scott Barrow, p. 27; Michael Brosilow, pp. 8, 9, 20, 25; Stock Boston/Bob
Deammrich, p. 5; PhotoEdit/Tony Freeman, p. 18; PhotoEdit/Robert Ginn, p. 21; Stock
Boston/Kevin Horan, p. 14; PhotoEdit/Bonnie Kamin, p. 22; PhotoEdit/Michael Newman,
pp. 7, 12, 16, 19, 29; Photodisc, p. 15; Stock Boston/Don Pitcher, p. 23; International Stock/Patrick
Ramsey, pp. 17, 28; Stock Boston, p.6; International Stock/Jay Thomas, p. 26; PhotoEdit/Dana
White, pp.4, 13; PhotoEdit/David Young-Wolfe, p. 24.

Illustration Tony Klassen, pp. 10–11.

Every effort has been made to contact copyright holders of any material reproduced in this
book. Any omissions will be rectified in subsequent printings if notice is given to the publisher.

Some words are shown in **bold**, like this.
You can find out what they mean by looking in the glossary.

# Contents

# Spending Without Cash

Did you know that it's possible to go shopping without **cash?** Banks offer services to their customers that let them buy things without using coins or paper money. These services include checks and special **bank cards.** Checks and bank cards can be used to buy things.

**A check is a note that tells the bank to pay some of the person's money to someone else.**

**There are many kinds of bank cards.**

In some ways, it is safer to use checks or bank cards to buy things. If money gets lost or stolen, there is no way to tell whom it belongs to. Checks and bank cards have the owner's name on them. Only that person can easily use them.

# Opening a Checking Account

One way to pay for things without money is by using a check. To do this, a person must have a **checking account.** To open a checking account, the customer gives the bank some money. This is called a **deposit.**

**This woman is opening a checking account.**

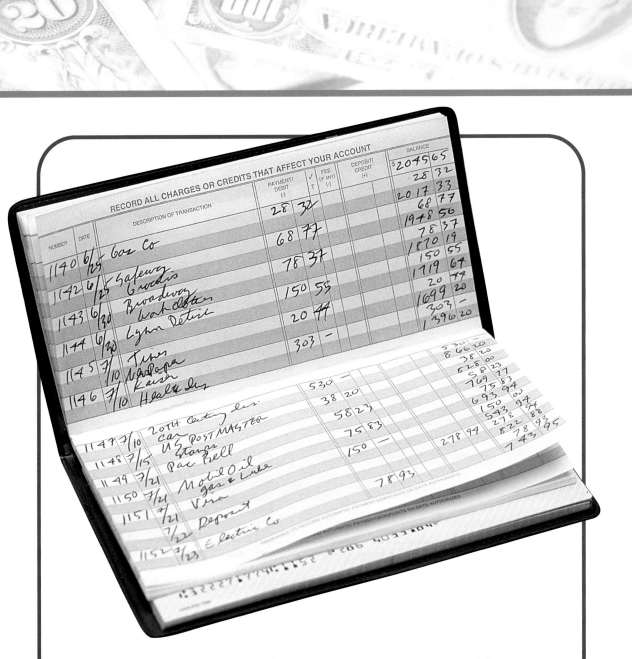

The bank gives every checking account owner a booklet of checks and a check register.

The checks can be used like money. Every time the person uses a check, he or she records the information in the **check register.** That way, the person knows how much money is left in the account.

# Paying by Check

Checks have information printed on them. The account owner's name and address is printed in one corner and the number of the check in another. There is also an **account number** that tells the bank whose **checking account** the checks go with.

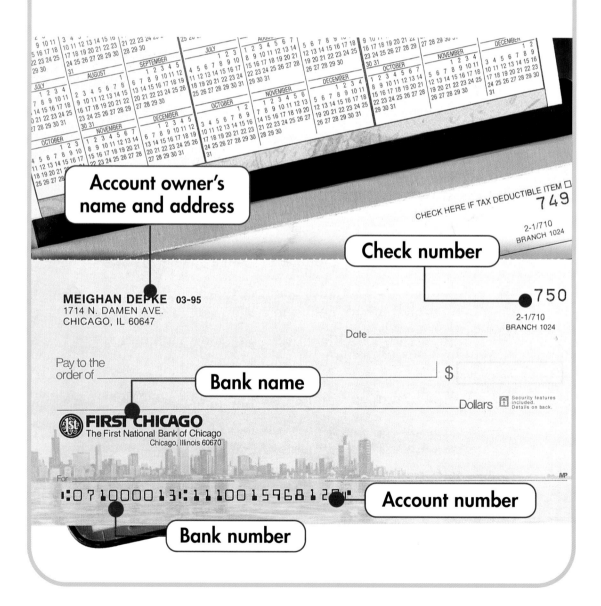

Account owner's name and address

CHECK HERE IF TAX DEDUCTIBLE ITEM ☐

749

2-1/710
BRANCH 1024

Check number

MEIGHAN DEPKE  03-95
1714 N. DAMEN AVE.
CHICAGO, IL 60647

750

2-1/710
BRANCH 1024

Date

Pay to the order of

Bank name

$

Dollars  Security features included. Details on back.

(S) **FIRST CHICAGO**
The First National Bank of Chicago
Chicago, Illinois 60670

For

MP

⑈071 0000 131⑈ 1 1 100 15968 12⑈

Account number

Bank number

**Amount written in numbers and in words**

**Person or company being paid**

**Date**

**Signature**

749

CHECK HERE IF TAX DEDUCTIBLE ITEM ☐

2-1/710
BRANCH 1024

750

2-1/710
BRANCH 1024

Date 9-30-99

CHICAGO, IL 60647

Pay to the order of _The Electric Company_ $ 35.00

_Thirty five dollars_ ∞ Dollars 🔒 Security features included. Details on back.

**FIRST CHICAGO**
The First National Ba... ...cago
Chicago,

For ⑈:07 10000 13⑈: 11 1... 129⑈ 0750

**All the blanks on this check have been filled in.**

A check is like a note telling the bank to pay someone else. But first, all the blank spaces have to be filled in. The account owner also has to put his or her **signature** at the bottom of the check.

9

# What Happens to a Check?

Do you know what happens to a check after it is written? Here's the story of one check.

1. Anthony writes a check for $50 to pay for groceries.

2. The store sends the check to its bank.

3. The bank sends the check to the **clearinghouse** that keeps track of its business.

4. That clearinghouse sends the check to the clearinghouse used by Anthony's bank.

5. The second clearinghouse sends the check to Anthony's bank. Fifty dollars is **deducted,** or subtracted, from his account.

6. Anthony's bank sends $50 to the store's bank. The money is **deposited** into the store's account.

7. The check, a copy of it, or a statement is sent back to Anthony. He knows the store has been paid.

# Debit Cards

People can use the money in their **checking accounts** without writing checks. They do this with a **debit card.** The numbers on the card tell whose checking account the card goes with. The card also has the account owner's name and **signature**.

A debit card can be used instead of a check.

**Debit card owners must keep track of their checking accounts so they don't spend more money than what they really have.**

Some businesses prefer to have customers use debit cards. To use a debit card, the person must have money in his or her account. Sometimes the bank will pay the store even if there isn't enough money. If that happens, the bank gets the money from the account owner and charges an extra **fee.**

# How Debit Cards Work

Every **debit card** has a magnetic strip on the back. The strip has a computer code in it. The debit card goes through a special machine at the store. This machine is hooked up to the bank's computers. They read the code and **deduct** the money from the person's **checking account.** The computers also send the money to the store's bank account.

**High-speed computers let stores and businesses check checking account information almost instantly.**

Businesses must pay banks a **fee** every time a customer uses a debit or credit card to pay for a purchase.

Then the machine prints out a **receipt** that shows how much the item cost. The person who owns the card has to sign the receipt. The clerk checks the **signature** and the one on the card to make sure they match.

# Checking a Checkbook

Every month, the bank sends each customer a **bank statement.** It shows everything that happened with the person's money that month. It lists all the checks that came back to the bank to be paid. It also lists purchases made with a **debit card**. Checks and debit card purchases are **deducted** from the person's **checking account**.

**Bank statements are mailed to customers every month.**

The amount of money in the bank statement and the **check register** should match.

The statement shows every **deposit** made to the checking account, too. These are added to the account. The statement shows how much money is still in the checking account. It is important to look over a bank statement carefully to be sure that there are no mistakes.

# Buy Now and Pay Later

People can buy things without using **cash,** checks, or **debit cards**. They can buy things even when they don't have the money to pay for them right away. Buying things this way is called "buying on **credit**." It is like getting a **loan**. The money has to be paid back later.

To get a debit or credit card, a person must have a record showing that he or she pays **bills** on time.

**Banks and credit card companies offer special cards to customers.**

To buy things on credit, people use another special card called a credit card. It is used like a debit card, but the money doesn't come from a **checking account.** Every credit card has a **credit limit.** This tells how much the customer can spend before paying some money back.

# Credit Cards

Many banks give **credit** cards to their customers. There are also credit card companies that offer cards. A credit card looks like a **debit card**. On the front it has the name of the bank or credit card company, a special **account number**, and the customer's name. On the back, it has a magnetic strip and the account owner's **signature**.

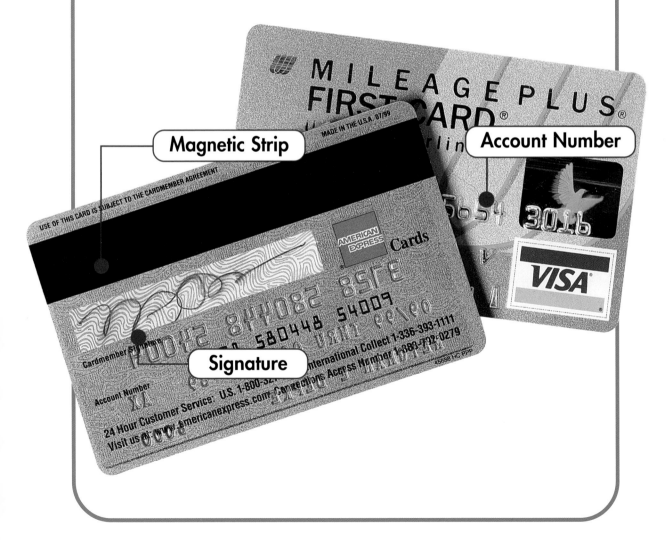

Magnetic Strip

Account Number

Signature

**Card owners must report lost credit cards to the bank or credit card company.**

It is important to keep track of debit and credit cards. If one gets lost or stolen, the bank or credit card company must be told. That way, no one else can try to use the card.

# How Credit Cards Work

Like a **debit card,** a **credit** card goes through a small machine. The machine reads the code on the back of the card and prints out a **receipt.** The credit card owner signs the receipt and the store clerk checks the **signature**.

**The signature on the receipt must match the signature on the card. If it doesn't, the store clerk won't complete the sale.**

**The credit card owner must check the bill carefully to make sure he or she has been charged the correct amount.**

The store keeps one copy of the receipt and the customer keeps another. The store sends its copy to the bank or credit card company. They pay the money to the store. Once a month, the credit card owner gets a **bill.** The bill lists all the purchases made with the credit card.

# Interest

A **credit** card owner can pay the whole **bill** at once or just part of it. The amount paid right away is the payment. The amount left over is the **balance**.

**This woman is writing a check to pay her credit card bill.**

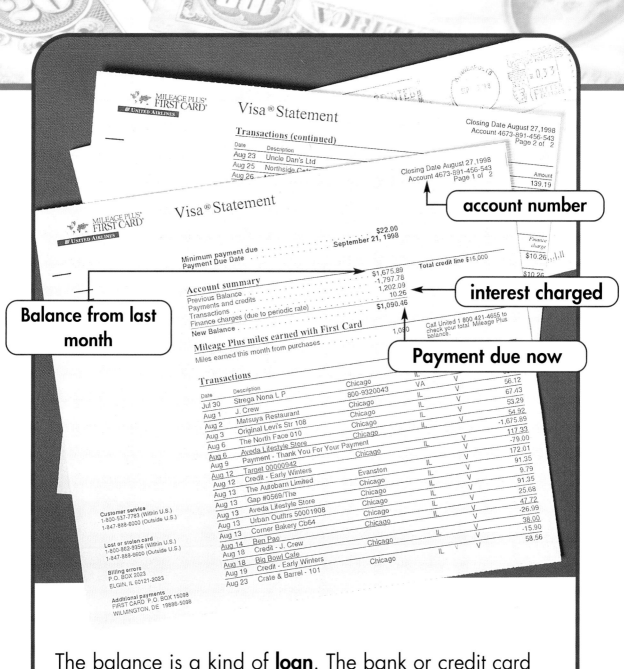

account number

interest charged

Balance from last month

Payment due now

**Visa® Statement**

MILEAGE PLUS
FIRST CARD
UNITED AIRLINES

Transactions (continued)

| Date | Description |
|------|-------------|
| Aug 23 | Uncle Dan's Ltd |
| Aug 25 | Northside Ca... |
| Aug 26 | ... |

Closing Date August 27, 1998
Account 4673-891-456-543
Page 2 of 2

| Amount |
|--------|
| 139.19 |

**Visa® Statement**

MILEAGE PLUS
FIRST CARD
UNITED AIRLINES

Closing Date August 27, 1998
Account 4673-891-456-543
Page 1 of 2

Minimum payment due          $22.00
Payment Due Date        September 21, 1998

Total credit line $15,000

Finance charge $10.26

$10.26

**Account summary**

| | |
|---|---|
| Previous Balance | $1,675.89 |
| Payments and credits | -1,797.78 |
| Transactions | 1,202.09 |
| Finance charges (due to periodic rate) | 10.26 |
| New Balance | $1,090.46 |

Mileage Plus miles earned with First Card          1,090

Miles earned this month from purchases

Call United 1 800 421-4655 to check your total Mileage Plus balance.

**Transactions**

| Date | Description | | | | Amount |
|------|-------------|---|---|---|--------|
| Jul 30 | Strega Nona L P | Chicago | VA | V | 56.12 |
| Aug 1 | J. Crew | 800-9320043 | IL | V | 67.43 |
| Aug 2 | Matsuya Restaurant | Chicago | IL | V | 53.29 |
| Aug 3 | Original Levi's Str 108 | Chicago | IL | V | 54.92 |
| Aug 6 | The North Face 010 | Chicago | IL | | -1,675.89 |
| Aug 6 | Aveda Lifestyle Store | Chicago | | V | 117.33 |
| Aug 9 | Payment - Thank You For Your Payment | | IL | V | -79.00 |
| Aug 12 | Target 00000942 | Chicago | | V | 172.01 |
| Aug 12 | Credit - Early Winters | | IL | V | 91.35 |
| Aug 13 | The Autobarn Limited | Evanston | IL | V | 9.79 |
| Aug 13 | Gap #0569/The | Chicago | IL | V | 91.35 |
| Aug 13 | Aveda Lifestyle Store | Chicago | IL | V | 25.68 |
| Aug 13 | Urban Outfitrs 50001908 | Chicago | IL | V | 47.72 |
| Aug 13 | Corner Bakery Cb64 | Chicago | | V | -26.99 |
| Aug 14 | Ben Pao | | IL | V | 38.00 |
| Aug 18 | Credit - J. Crew | Chicago | | V | -15.90 |
| Aug 18 | Big Bowl Cafe | | IL | V | 58.56 |
| Aug 19 | Credit - Early Winters | Chicago | | V | |
| Aug 23 | Crate & Barrel - 101 | | | | |

Customer service
1-800-537-7783 (Within U.S.)
1-847-888-6000 (Outside U.S.)

Lost or stolen card
1-800-862-9356 (Within U.S.)
1-847-888-6600 (Outside U.S.)

Billing errors
P.O. BOX 2023
ELGIN, IL 60121-2023

Additional payments
FIRST CARD P.O. BOX 15098
WILMINGTON, DE 19886-5098

The balance is a kind of **loan**. The bank or credit card company lets the account owner borrow the money, but it charges a **fee** for this service. This fee is called **interest**, and it is added to the person's next bill. The longer it takes to pay a bill completely, the more interest the person will end up paying. So it is smart to pay the the total amount of the bill as quickly as possible.

# Debt

A **debt** is money owed to someone. A **credit** card **balance** is a kind of debt. There are other types of debts. Most people don't have enough money to pay for a house, car, or college education all at once. They borrow money from a bank or **loan** company.

**Many people use loans to help pay for college. They will pay back the loan after college, when they have jobs.**

**This woman is checking to see how much interest she owes.**

Like any other debt, credit card debt must be paid back. The money doesn't have to be paid all at once. However, **interest** is added to the amount owed. The longer it takes to pay, the more interest is charged. Interest adds up quickly. It makes debts harder to pay back. So it's important to use credit cards wisely.

# Using Credit Wisely

One way to use **credit** wisely is not to use it too often. Another is to pay credit card **debts** quickly. Everyone has certain "needs." Food, clothing, transportation, and a place to live are all examples of things people must buy.

**Families must spend quite a bit of money for food.**

**Wants are things like vacations, fancy cars, restaurant meals, or even expensive perfumes.**

Everyone also has "wants." These are things people can get along without, but might like to have or do. People need to make wise choices about how they spend money. That way they won't go into **debt** for things they don't need.

# Glossary

**account number**  number that tells to whom a bank account belongs

**balance**  amount of money still owed

**bank card**  plastic card given by a bank to a customer

**bank statement**  written record of what happens to the money a person keeps in the bank

**bill**  piece of paper that tells how much someone owes at a certain time

**cash**  coins and paper money

**check register**  booklet for keeping track of how checks are used

**checking account**  service offered by a bank that lets people use money without carrying cash

**clearinghouse**  business that helps a bank take care of its money

**credit limit**  total amount of money a person can borrow

**credit**  to be able buy something with borrowed money

**debit card**  bank card that lets someone pay for something with money in a checking account

**debt**  money owed to someone else

**deduct** to take away or subtract

**deposit** to put money into a bank account

**fee** money charged for a service

**interest** fee charged for borrowing money; or money paid to people for letting someone else use their money

**loan** money someone borrows

**payment** amount of a bill that is paid at one time

**receipt** written record of how much something cost or how much a person spent

**signature** person's full name written by that person

# More Books to Read

Armentrout, Patricia. *Paying Without Money.* Vero Beach: Fla.: Rourke Publishers, 1996.

Moose, Christina J. *Budgeting.* Vero Beach, Fla.: Rourke Publishers, 1997.

Moose, Christina J. *Debt.* Vero Beach, Fla.: Rourke Publishers, 1997.

# Index